I Belong to the Hindu Faith

Katie Dicker and Alka Vekaria

PowerKiDS
press.

New York

Published in 2010 by The Rosen Publishing Group Inc.
29 East 21st Street, New York, NY 10010

Copyright © 2010 Wayland/The Rosen Publishing Group, Inc.

First Edition

Library of Congress Cataloging-in-Publication Data

Dicker, Katie
   I belong to the Hindu faith / Katie Dicker and Alka Vekaria.
      p. cm. -- (I belong)
   Includes index.
   ISBN 978-1-4358-3033-2 (library binding)
   ISBN 978-1-4358-8620-9 (paperback)
   ISBN 978-1-4358-8621-6 (6-pack)
   1. Religious life--Hinduism--Juvenile literature. I. Vekaria, Alka II. Title.
   BL1237.32.D53 2010
   294.5--dc22

                                    2008051877

Manufactured in China

Disclaimer
The text in this book is based on the experience of one family. Although every effort
has been made to offer accurate and clearly expressed information, the author and
publisher acknowledge that some explanations may not be relevant to those who
practice their faith in a different way.

Acknowledgements
The author and publisher would like to thank the following people for their help and
participation in this book:
The Vekaria family, Liz Bayram, Louise Banks, and Kirti Kothari.

Photography by Chris Fairclough.

Contents

A celebration

Hi, I'm Alka, and this is my family—my mom and dad and my sister, Gopi. We're Hindus. Today, we're going to the **mandir** to celebrate the festival of **Diwali**.

We've put on our best clothes. I'm wearing a new **choli**, Mom and Gopi are wearing new **saris**, and Dad is wearing a **kurta pajama**.

The mandir is open every day for people to visit, pray, study, and celebrate Hindu holidays. There's a big prayer hall, a kitchen, a library, some classrooms, and a hall where we eat.

We go to the mandir to **worship**. The building looks a little bit like a palace—a special place for the gods to stay.

SHREE SWAMINARAYAN TEMPLE
UNDER N.N. DEV TEMPLE BHUJ

At the mandir

We go to the mandir to give thanks to God who created everything we see around us. God has also sent other gods and goddesses into the world to help us understand his goodness.

We take off our shoes at the mandir to show our respect to the gods. It's also to keep the mandir clean.

There are lots of ways of practicing the Hindu religion, and the gods we worship have different names. Vishnu was a god who came to earth in many forms. When he was human, he was named Lord Shree Krishna.

Lord Shree Krishna is often shown playing the flute. His skin is colored blue because his presence is never-ending—just like the blue sky.

Lord Shree Swaminarayan

God also came to Earth as Lord Shree Swaminarayan to teach people about **Hinduism** and how to live a good life. Our temple has a main **shrine** showing Lord Swaminarayan.

This statue of Lord Swaminarayan is made from marble. It shows him as a child when he was known as Shree Ghanshyam Maharaj.

Lord Shree Swaminarayan was born over 200 years ago. When he was eleven, he left home and began traveling through India. He helped to spread the teachings of our religion. Throughout his life, he performed miracles.

This scene reminds us of the time Lord Swaminarayan traveled through the forest as a child. It must have been very frightening when he was all alone.

How do we worship?

There are lots of pictures and statues of the gods for us to worship at the mandir. We can go there on any day, but we usually go on the weekend when we're not at school.

We ask the gods for guidance and we offer gifts to the statues. We also put our hands together or bow down to show our love and respect.

We all sit down and listen to stories about the gods. Afterward, we have an **Aarti** ceremony. We say prayers as we pass candles called **divas** around the room. The flame reminds us of God's light, warmth, and protection.

I move my hands over the diva and then pass my hands over my head. This makes me feel closer to God.

Diwali

Diwali is the festival of lights. It is based on the story of **Lord Rama's** return after defeating the evil king **Ravana**. People lit lamps to guide Rama on his way.

This beautiful food is called **Prashad**. It is being offered to the gods during Diwali. The food will then be shared with everyone.

Diwali also marks the start of our New Year, when we think about forgiveness and new beginnings. We've worked hard to fill the mandir with lights and decorations for our celebrations. It looks amazing!

This is a statue of the god, Ganesh. Ganesh helps to make the future easier for us. It's good to pray to him at the start of a new year.

Food and friends

My family don't eat meat. We believe animals feel pain as we do. Animals such as cows also give us milk and butter and should be cared for. God gives us our food, and we treat it with respect.

We all share a meal after we worship on festival days. It's traditional for men and women to sit on different sides of the room in the mandir.

After we've eaten, we have time to talk to everyone and catch up on their news. We love coming to the mandir—there are so many things to learn about our religion, and friends to see.

Our friends at the mandir are always looking out for us. It feels like we're part of the same family.

Praying at home

At home, we have pictures of the gods that we worship, such as Lord Swaminarayan and Ganesh. We pray to the gods and offer them gifts, such as water, food, flowers, or **incense**.

This shrine shows Lord Swaminarayan. We light a candle as we pray and cover our heads to show our respect.

Every morning after I wash and dress, I do my **Puja**. I pray to the gods to keep me safe and ask for their guidance if I need their help with something.

I lay down these **murtis** and I ring a bell to tell the gods I'm near. I also use prayer beads inside this bag to help me concentrate.

Learning from the scriptures

There are ancient Hindu books and scriptures that guide us in our lives. The oldest of these are called the Vedas—they contain the words of God.

The Vedas are songs and poems written in a language called Sanskrit. Mom is explaining what is written in the holy books.

I like to read the Shishapatri every day. This book is taken from the Hindu scriptures. The words teach me to respect others and to avoid evil, so I will be rewarded in the future.

Every morning, I put this dot on my forehead using a special red powder. It's called a chandlo. According to the scriptures, it guards me against evil.

Living a good life

Our religion teaches us that how we behave is more important than what we believe. There's a part of God inside each of our hearts. Every day, I try to reveal God's love in the things I do.

Gopi always helps me if I'm feeling down. I try to be kind to her, too, especially if she's had a busy day.

I think about God every day and thank him for the good things he has given me. I try to respect my elders and to live an honest life, as God would want me to.

I am learning **Gujarati** to help me read the Hindu scriptures. I try to work hard to use the skills God has given me.

Glossary, further information, and Web Sites

Aarti a special Hindu ceremony to remind people of God's power.

choli a short top and long skirt.

diva a candle made from twisted cotton soaked in a type of butter called ghee.

Gujarati a language spoken in parts of India.

Hinduism the Hindu religion.

incense a substance that is burned to produce a pleasant smell.

kurta pajama a tunic and pants.

Lord Rama a legendary king of ancient India.

mandir a building where Hindus go to worship God.

murtis images of Hindu gods and goddesses.

Prashad food that is shared after a Hindu service or festival.

Puja a form of prayer performed each morning.

Ravana an evil king who had ten heads and twenty hands.

sari a long piece of material wrapped around the body.

shrine a place where images of the gods are kept and worshipped.

worship to show love and respect to God.

Did you know?

- Hinduism is the world's oldest religion. It began in India about 5,000 years ago near the Indus river (in what is now called Pakistan). The people there were called Hindus.
- There are around 750 million Hindus in the world, mostly living in India.
- The dates of Hindu festivals follow a lunar calendar.

Activities

1. Find the name of a Hindu god you have not heard of before. Use books or the internet to find out the story about this god.
2. Make a card to celebrate Diwali.
3. Write a poem about the Hindu way of life.

Books to read

- *Rookie Read-About Holidays: Diwali* by Christina Mia Gardeski (Children's Press, 2001)
- *This is my Faith: Hinduism* by Anita Ganeri (Barron's Educational, 2006)
- *Traditional Religious Tales: Hindu Stories* by Anita Ganeri (Picture Window Books, 2006)

Web Sites

Due to the changing nature of Internet links, PowerKids Press has developed an online list of Web sites related to the subject of this book. This site is updated regularly. Please use this link to access this list: www.powerkidslinks.com/blong/hindu

Hindu festivals

Diwali (October/November)
The festival of lights, celebrating Rama's return. The Hindu New Year (**Ankut**) is also celebrated during Diwali.

Holi (February/March)
A festival when Hindus remember Lord Krishna. Bonfires are lit as a sign of the triumph of good over evil, and colored powders are thrown over people.

Ramnavmi (April)
Birthday of Lord Swaminarayan and Lord Rama.

Janmastimi (August)
Birthday of Lord Shree Krishna.

Dussehra (October)
A celebration of the triumph of good over evil. This festival reminds Hindus of when Rama defeated the evil king Ravana.

Hindu symbols

Aum the Hindu word for God. The Aum symbol represents life, death, and rebirth.

Hindu swastika symbol an ancient Hindu symbol of luck and good fortune.

Index